Letters
Granddaughter

A Memoir of My Life Told Through
125 Memory Prompts

Letters Written By:

_____

ABOUT THIS BOOK

Knowing how and where to begin your story can seem a daunting task after-all, you have seen so much in your lifetime. Letters to my Granddaughter solves this problem by providing you with 125 short prompts. As you read the prompts, memories and stories will flash up. These are the things that you share in the letters you will write in this book.

You might like to start with the first prompt "I am writing in this book because". Be honest, be real, and be yourself. The relationship between an author and the reader is an intimate one, and in your case, you know your granddaughter will be the one reading it. This is your chance to tell her things that you have not had the chance to tell her yet. Tell her exactly why you are starting this project and what you are hoping to achieve.

There are different types of prompts in this book, you will find quite specific prompts that direct your thoughts to a particular time in your life. You will also find prompts that are much wider – encouraging you to expand on what they bring up for you. These might be about your thoughts feelings or ideas.

At the back of this book, you will find several pages without prompts. These are for you to use if you need more space, or if you would like to include stories that you have not included elsewhere in your letters.

When it is time to write, flick through the prompts and find one that speaks to you. Stop there, go into your memory, and think for a couple of minutes before you begin to write your letter.

Share your feelings – she wants to know all about you and will love reading your letters.

Describe the scenes in as much detail as possible. Talk about how things look, the sounds you hear, what you can smell, and what things feel like.
Include those quirky little memories that pop up, the things that you remember vividly, but have no idea why they made such an impression on you.

When you are sharing about events, include who was there with you. Describe when it happened, the date, the time of day, the weather. Where exactly are you? How did you get there, when you look around, what can you see? What were you thinking before, during and after? Did the event change you in any way, did your ideas change, your knowledge, your personality?

Treat each prompt as its own little story. You know your story, everything is in your heart or your head. You know how it begins and how it ends. You know the important parts that you simply must include, and you also know the funny parts and the parts that made you cry.

Be natural, and tell your story as it comes to you.

Some people like to include life lessons – these are the things that you learned from the experience that you are sharing.

One of the best parts about this book is that you hand write your own story. The art of handwriting is being lost with the advent of computers and printers. Having a book full of your stories in your handwriting will be an absolute treasure for generations to come. So even if you think your handwriting is messy or uneven, please let that go right now. See the beauty in it – for your handwriting is beautiful and it is wholly yours.

I am writing in this book because

A holiday memory

Fun things I did when I was a child

My first boyfriend

I remember crying

The part of my life that I look back on with the most fondness

A summer holiday memory

When I was a child I got into trouble for

_____

_____

_____

_____

_____

_____

_____

_____

_____

_____

_____

_____

_____

_____

_____

_____

_____

My first home

My favorite subject in school

My bedroom when I was a child

_____

_____

_____

_____

_____

_____

_____

_____

_____

_____

_____

_____

_____

_____

_____

_____

_____

_____

_____

If I could travel back in time for a week, I would

Getting older

Prom

My career

I wish that

A spring memory

Books I have read that I love

_____
_____
_____
_____
_____
_____
_____
_____
_____
_____
_____
_____
_____
_____
_____
_____
_____
_____
_____
_____

I was there when

I am most proud of

My favorite movie

A chance encounter

I made a

My wildest party

_____
_____
_____
_____
_____
_____
_____
_____
_____
_____
_____
_____
_____
_____
_____
_____
_____
_____
_____

My best memory as a teenager with my friends

New Year's Eve in 19_ _

My favorite flower

A secret from my childhood

My hobbies when I was a teenager

The best day of my life

I survived

_____

_____

_____

_____

_____

_____

_____

_____

_____

_____

_____

_____

_____

_____

_____

_____

_____

_____

_____

_____

I never thought I would

_____

_____

_____

_____

_____

_____

_____

_____

_____

_____

_____

_____

_____

_____

_____

_____

_____

Someone close to me died

The food we ate when I was a child

When I was 10 I wanted to

My most vivid memory from school

_____

_____

_____

_____

_____

_____

_____

_____

_____

_____

_____

_____

_____

_____

_____

_____

_____

_____

My favorite place in the world

The most difficult choice I ever had to make

The best gift I have ever received

Love is

My most beloved toy

_____

_____

_____

_____

_____

_____

_____

_____

_____

_____

_____

_____

_____

_____

_____

_____

_____

I failed at

My family came from

My greatest success

My neighborhood when I was a childhood

My earliest memory

An autumn memory

Mom's kitchen

Now I know

When I saw you for the first time

My favorite people

The greatest challenge of my life

_____

_____

_____

_____

_____

_____

_____

_____

_____

_____

_____

_____

_____

_____

_____

_____

_____

_____

_____

_____

_____

What I wish I knew at 20

I wish I could show you

A favorite childhood hideaway

The first few weeks of being a new mother

_____

_____

_____

_____

_____

_____

_____

_____

_____

_____

_____

_____

_____

_____

_____

_____

_____

Stories my parents told me

My heroes are

My first best friend

A conversation that I remember

Life is

An interesting relative

Family traditions from my childhood

The person I wish I could re-connect with

A favorite memory of my child/children

My collection

The place that I feel is home

A memory about a pet or animal

_____

_____

_____

_____

_____

_____

_____

_____

_____

_____

_____

_____

_____

_____

_____

_____

_____

_____

Cooking

My grandfather

The naughtiest thing I ever did

My religious journey

Where and when I was born

If I could live my life again I would

People who have inspired me

An important friendship

Competitions I have won

My first day of school

_____
_____
_____
_____
_____
_____
_____
_____
_____
_____
_____
_____
_____
_____
_____
_____
_____
_____
_____
_____

My first car

The most amazing natural event that I have seen

_____

_____

_____

_____

_____

_____

_____

_____

_____

_____

_____

_____

_____

_____

_____

_____

_____

The naughtiest thing your mother or father did when they were a child

My first job

School was

_____

_____

_____

_____

_____

_____

_____

_____

_____

_____

_____

_____

_____

_____

_____

_____

_____

_____

_____

A childhood injury or illness

When I was 35 I wanted

A winter memory

Being pregnant was

My first kiss

_____

_____

_____

_____

_____

_____

_____

_____

_____

_____

_____

_____

_____

_____

_____

_____

_____

_____

_____

_____

My beliefs as a teenager

How I met your grandfather

I wish I could have learned more in school about

My father loved

My scariest memory

I have always wanted to go to

_____

_____

_____

_____

_____

_____

_____

_____

_____

_____

_____

_____

_____

_____

_____

_____

_____

Becoming an adult

When I was 15 I wanted to

_____

_____

_____

_____

_____

_____

_____

_____

_____

_____

_____

_____

_____

_____

_____

_____

_____

_____

_____

I felt like a hero when

A historical event that impacted me

My favorite restaurant

A funny memory about your mother or father

_____

_____

_____

_____

_____

_____

_____

_____

_____

_____

_____

_____

_____

_____

_____

_____

_____

_____

When I was 25 I wanted to

A time I was fired or quit my job

My favorite food

I once hated, but now like

My favorite teacher at school

My grandmother

My best friend

Most unusual place I have lived

_____

_____

_____

_____

_____

_____

_____

_____

_____

_____

_____

_____

_____

_____

_____

_____

_____

_____

A family heirloom

My first heartbreak

A sport or game

My life goals

A memory of ice cream

My favorite childhood memory

I moved out of my parents' house when

My most treasured memory

_____

_____

_____

_____

_____

_____

_____

_____

_____

_____

_____

_____

_____

_____

_____

_____

_____

_____

_____

6 people (living or dead) I would invite to dinner

The home I remember the most

I have a talent that you don't know about

My life changed when

Money is

A song that brings back good memories

My mother loved

When I was 12 I thought that

I want to tell you that